W9-CNQ-607

Shaesn.

Stop + Listen~
Erin Campbell

HARK

North Productions

Published by North Productions
www.erincampbellstories.com

Printed by LifeTouch Publishing
5126 Forest Hills Court
Loves Park, IL 61111

Text copyright © 2013 by Erin Campbell
Illustrations copyright © 2013 by Shannon Sutton

Edited by Meghan Snare
Designed by Aaron Campbell

All rights reserved. No part of this publication may be reproduced or transmitted
in any form or by any means, electronic or mechanical, including photocopying,
recording, or any information storage and retrieval system, without permission
in writing from the publisher, except in the case of brief quotations embodied
in critical articles or reviews.

Text type is set in Century Schoolbook

First Edition

Made in Rockford, IL

ISBN: 978-0-9911576-0-0

To Jack -
May you have a sensitive spirit, an
obedient heart, an agile mind, and a strong backbone
to stand up for truth and justice. I love being
your mom. You are the heart of my heart.

To Libby, Brady, and Ethan -
Honored to be on the road less traveled with you.

To Aaron -
I couldn't, and wouldn't, do this without you.

Hark

Written by Erin Campbell
Illustrated by Shannon Sutton

Once upon a time, not so long ago, there was a busy town full of busy people who had busy things to do. God had messages for these people, and since He knew getting their attention would take special dedication, He summoned Hark, His newest messenger angel.

Hark was excited and a little nervous, too. This was his first big assignment. When Hark was in training he had seen first-hand the difference God's words could make.

To Joshua, God said, "March around the city seven times. On the seventh time, as the trumpets blow, have all the people shout a great shout and the city walls will fall down flat."

To David, God spoke, "I will guide you along the best pathway for your life. I will advise you and watch over you."

Hark was there when God's first messenger whispered, "Fear not."

To the people of Israel the message was sent, "Don't be discouraged, for I am your God. I will strengthen you and help you. I will hold you up with my victorious right hand."

And Hark would never forget the moment these words echoed across time and space, took Mary's breath away, and changed everything.

"Name him Jesus [God Saves] because he will save his people from their sins."

Heart thumping, Hark landed before God.

Hark wondered what messages he would be sent to deliver.
Direction for a big decision? Provision for a pressing
need? Assurance that all would be well? No matter
what the messages were, Hark knew they would
be important. Every message from God is.

"What are Your messages, Lord?"

Hark trembled in anticipation of the weight of each word
from God. God smiled. His eyes twinkled.

Hark bowed his head, ready to receive God's messages.

God placed his hand on Hark's lowered head and spoke the words Hark was to deliver.

A smile spread across Hark's face and with a nod and a flash of wings, Hark was on his way.

The house was anything but quiet when Hark arrived. Hark waited for the television to be turned off and for the dryer to buzz. He waited for teeth to be brushed and faces to be washed. He waited for closets and dark corners to be checked for monsters, he waited for lullabies to be sung and waited some more as the baby boy was tucked into his crib. Hark waited for sweet dreams and deep sleep. Hark waited for quiet.

At last, Hark leaned over the baby's crib. The little one cooed at the angel, unafraid. The two locked eyes and Hark softly delivered his first message.

"No matter how it feels, you will never be alone."

The baby took a deep breath and fell into a restful sleep.

When Hark arrived to deliver his
second message, he found Grandma
as he usually did, sitting in her
rocking chair rocking and
praying, praying and rocking.
For this message Hark didn't
have to wait. He spread
his wings over Grandma
and said,

"I have heard you and
I am at work."

The rocking stopped.
A tear rolled down
Grandma's cheek.

"Thank you Lord, thank you."

Hark's next message was more difficult to deliver. The rush of activity was non-stop. Days filled with bus rides, hallways, classrooms, soccer practices, texts, pictures, music. All the while Hark had to be patient because this message was too important to get mixed up in the noise.

Late one night Hark saw his opportunity.

The boy was sprawled across his bed where he had been listening to music and doing homework. Hark knew this was the right moment. Just as the charge on the music player faded, Hark pulled up one of the headphones and said,

"No one besides your Creator may determine your identity. And He says you are good."

The boy tensed at the sound of Hark, but quickly relaxed. The boy nodded his head, stretched, and confidently went back to work.

Hark could not imagine a more meaningful existence! With beating wings he flew off to deliver message, after message, after message.

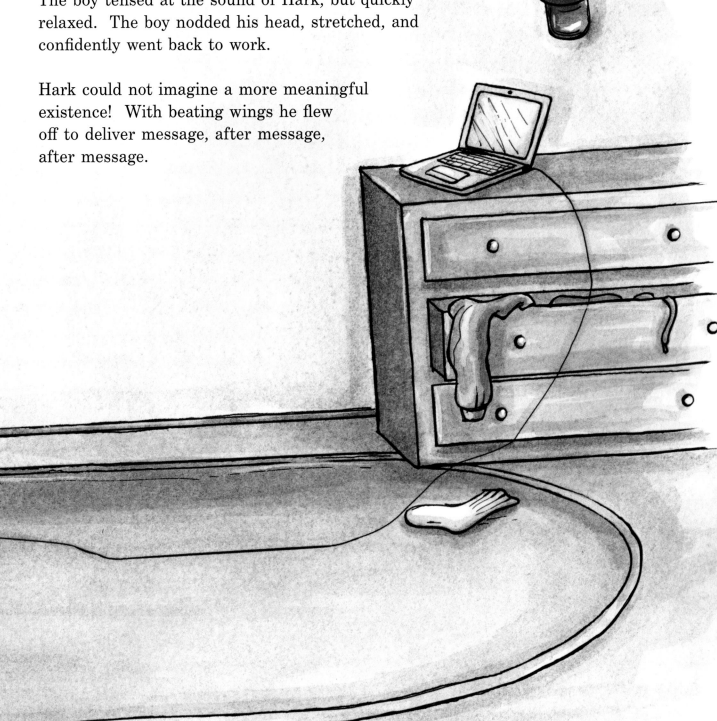

"I did not cause this and I am going to get you through it."

"I can use just who you are and just what you have to make a difference in this world."

"I made this for you because I love you."

"I will give you the courage, strength, and wisdom to do the right thing."

"I am real, I am good, and I can be trusted."

Hark flew through the town's streets. The people were so busy, their lives so loud. Hark saw how each day was filled with distraction, noise, and different kinds of messages.

How would the people remember God's messages amongst the rest? Hark knew he had to do something to help the people never forget their messages.

Hark had a familiar thumping in his chest. He knew how important it was for each person to hear and remember the words of God. Hark understood the potential God's words had to change the course of each life.

Hark flew directly to God.

"What is on your mind, Hark?" God asked.

"How will the people tell the difference between Your messages and all the other messages they are flooded with? Even if they receive the right message, how will they remember it?"

God replied, "Do you have any ideas?"

"There is a fountain in the park at the center of town. The fountain isn't very large and it isn't very ornate, but all the streets lead to it. As I was delivering Your messages I saw that many people come to sit in this park. Even those who don't stay at least look at the fountain as they go by...."

God knew the plan that had formed in the heart of Hark. It was a good plan, so God simply responded, "Yes."

With a snap of his wings Hark was gone.

Hark tilted and swooped and spiraled through the cool of the night, moving his powerful wings for the last time. Each mighty beat brought Hark closer to the fulfillment of his plan. He dove for the fountain. At the last second, Hark spread open his wings and landed firmly in the center.

"God, may this help them remember."

Then Hark froze.

The next morning people were rushing about as
they usually did, until they passed by the park.

"What a wonderful sculpture!"

"Who made it?"

"Where did it come from?"

"You know, it looks kind of familiar..."

A single message was carved into the statue:

"Remember."

If you pass a city square
And see an angel standing there,

Pause and listen.

Your heart will feel a sudden thrill,
For God is sending messages still.

Author's Note:

To everyone who has taught me to be still and listen,
thank you. Our world is chaotic at times and we have,
in part, lost the art of listening. It is hard to clearly
hear the messages God is sending when we are
never still, never quiet, never open.

Be still, be quiet, and be open, for God has a message
for you. He is patient and He will send His messages
again and again; just don't miss them forever.

To those of you who have heard God's messages
once upon a time, pause and remember.